ANXIOUS MOMENTS

ANXIOUS MOMENTS

POEMS BY ALEŠ DEBELJAK

.

TRANSLATED FROM THE SLOVENE BY
CHRISTOPHER MERRILL
(WITH THE AUTHOR)

PREFACE BY CHARLES SIMIC

WHITE PINE PRESS • FREDONIA, NY

Acknowledgements:
Some of the translations in this volume have appeared in
*The Case of Slovenia, Double Vision: Four Slovenian Poets,
Poetry International, The Prose Poem: An International Journal*
and *Redlands Review.*

Publication of this book was made possible, in part,
by grants from the National Endowment for the Arts,
the New York State Council on the Arts,
and the Trubar Foundation.

Cover photograph of Aleš Debeljak by Jani Straus

Book design by Watershed Design

Printed in the United States of America

ISBN 1-877727-35-0

1 2 3 4 5 6 7 8 9

WHITE PINE PRESS
10 Village Square
Fredonia, New York 14063

for you, maybe

CONTENTS

ANXIOUS MOMENTS

TRANSLATOR'S INTRODUCTION

Aleš Debeljak was born in 1961 in Ljubljana, the capital of Slovenia, which was until 1991 the northernmost republic of Yugoslavia. Educated at the University of Ljubljana and Syracuse University in New York, in the 1980s Debeljak established himself as the leading young literary figure in Slovenia, a land with a population of two million. In a short period of time he produced a remarkable body of work: four collections of poetry, three books of cultural criticism, and countless reviews, articles, and essays. In 1990 he received the Prešeren Prize — the Slovenian National Book Award — and now he teaches cultural studies at the University of Ljubljana.

His literary models? It is a commonplace to say that Slovenians seek inspiration either from Venice or from Vienna, and Debeljak inclines toward the latter. Rainier Maria Rilke, Paul Celan, Georg Trakl — these are the Germanic masters hovering behind his melancholic poems. Yet *Anxious Moments* is the work of a wholly original artist. Debeljak writes poetry in bursts, completing an entire book in a matter of weeks, then falling silent for months and even years. It is as though he makes a long journey into the woods of his imagination, returns with a cycle of poems, and then rests up for his next poetic adventure — a break, it should be noted, filled with prose writings on a variety of literary and political subjects.

Debeljak's prose poems are marked by his razor-sharp intelligence, haunting juxtapositions, and imagery which is at once slightly surreal and rooted in Slovenian life and folklore. *Anxious Moments* is a book of promptings and premonitions, and it was not until the advent of the Ten-Day War between Slovenia and Yugoslavia that the full dimensions of this book became apparent. Composed more than a year and a half before the war, nevertheless *Anxious Moments* is teeming with the exiles, nomads, and burned villages that have since become a staple of the nightly news from the Balkans. These are the poems of a writer who in at least one respect foresaw the future: a troubling collection of glimpses into the abyss opening even then in what we would soon call the former Yugoslavia.

Certainly I was troubled by these poems when in February 1991 Aleš and I rendered them into English. Our method of translation resembled his composition of the book itself: over the course of five days in my flat in New Orleans, working twelve to fourteen hours at a stretch, we translated all of *Anxious Moments*. Because I knew no Slovenian, Aleš provided me with a rough English version of his book, and from these notes I tried to write poems, asking my friend at every turn to explain the sound, meaning, and imagery of his original work. It was a time of feverish and nerve-wracking activity unlike anything I had ever experienced, and for months afterwards the poems disconcerted me. That summer, however, their mysterious glow became the first of the fires the world continues to watch in horror. These are the *Anxious Moments* of a poet who knew in his bones that the new world order would be anything but orderly, which makes his poems ever more frightening – and true.

PREFACE

In the beginning was the epic and the folk song. Then came the lyric poem. Someone said, "I exist," and wondered that it should be so. The world hasn't been the same since. Lyric poetry remains the place where the individual asserts himself or herself against the gods and demons of history and the tribe. In that sense the lyric poem remains potentially the most subversive of literary forms. It sings of love in time of war and prefers the loved one undressed to the sight of chariots and heroes arrayed for battle. Its secret ambition is philosophical. The lyric poem is the place where passion and metaphysics meet.

"Do you recognize yourself in this poem?"

Aleš Debeljak asks. It's a question all lyric poets ask. And the answer is yes, from time to time we recognize ourselves, to our great surprise, even in a poem by a thousand-year-old Chinese poet. Memory, solitude, love, exile and return, are all there. In a lyric poem everything and everyone comes together. The prose poem is the most outrageous example of this. Fable, legends, creation myth, bedtime story, travel journal, epistle, diary, dream are just some of its ingredients. The prose poem reads like a narrative, but works like a lyric since it relies on juxtaposition of images and unexpected turns of phrase. An interrupted narrative, it insists that it has to be read over and over again until its words and images radiate their full mystery. A prose poem, the way Debeljak writes it, is an invitation to the imagination; every poem a new adventure in a new world.

"Anxious Moments" is an appropriate title. These are moments of consciousness, moments of anxious sense of one's own mortality, times when we say with Debeljak:

"This moment won't pass. Ever."

The surprise of what comes together, things and faces, a moment which has a way of haunting our entire life from then on. "Metaphor, yearning, the whole world," Debeljak says. Of course. In that moment of consciousness the laws of our being are to be discovered. In that sense the modern poem is epistomological. Every poem is a critical act, a phenomenology of the spirit.

Debeljak has also spoken of an influence of American poetry on his own. What American poetry offers, what may be its most attractive characteristic is an almost total disregard for the separation of the language of prose and poetry. Even more than that, no one mixes literary and colloquial languages the way Americans do. An American poem, Pound's Cantos or something by Ashbery, is a quilt of various levels and types of dictions. Everything is there, from latinate phrases, philosophical and scientific vocabularies to plain realistic prose and street slang. Since the main literary project everywhere and in every age is how to renew the lyric, the way the best American poetry uses all the resources of language can come in handy. That influence is more visible in Debeljak's poems in verse, than in his prose poetry but it's there, too, in the enormous freedom with which he incorporates seemingly incongruous verbal elements. What holds all this together is the emotion. All true lyric poets are exiles. This is a book of tiny odes and elegies. And they are beautiful.

The poet who is not sensitive to the enormity and complexity of our historical and intellectual predicament is not worth reading. Debeljak fulfills that difficult task. "In this strange universe where one is a stranger," says Melville. How true that seems again! Debeljak comes from a small country that has given birth to many great poets. Edvard Kocbek and Tomaž Šalumun are, perhaps, the best known in the West. They too share that awe at the strangeness of our predicament.

And so the poems: a few words surrounded by much silence, and my sense while reading Debeljak, that this is what pondering one's life feels like in this waning century.

— Charles Simic

ANXIOUS MOMENTS

ELEGIES FROM THE NORTH

Earth. Red earth. And tall grass as far as you can see. You're pressed to the ground. Hidden from unwanted glances. Utterly still. A quail by your ear. Are you turning into stone? No: you're just listening to shadows fall over cornfields. A bead of sweat — a tear? — slides down your cheek. In the distance a mountain rises steeply. Naked. Without trees or flowers. Imprinted on the sharp-edged horizon. On its peak, lost in the clouds, generations of stag hunters wander for centuries. Glistening of the setting sun. All the signs say: end of Indian summer. If I hear it right, nothing comes from your lips. Are you dumb? Blind? Perhaps you're searching through memory for the shapes of all prints — footsteps in the snow, old songs and cognac in the evening, small white towns with castles and turrets, the smells of Sunday afternoons, the river running under granite bridges. As if this, too, escapes you. Here, under the empty sky of ancient tribes you never heard about, you'll end your way. I, of course, always return. You don't. Which makes all the difference.

The sodden moss sinks underfoot when we cross half-frozen bays and walk through birch groves, wandering in an uneven circle that widens into darkness, through the minds and bodies of men and animals trapped in last year's snow — no: trapped from the beginning, emptiness all around us, ice collecting on our pale faces, I can hear you singing on the run, an unknown melody, I can't make out the words, clouds of breath freeze on your fur collar, eyes open wide as we trudge through silence and weakening starlight, through the fevered babble of children exiled to distant camps, insects curling up under bark, December or June, no difference, ashes blanket the ground as far as you can see, damp wool of shirts, we wade through the fog rolling in from the hills, oozing into our lungs, hills where there must be flowers about to bloom under a woman's eyelids, who dreams of dark faces hardening into granite, the snow's covering us, we're asleep on our feet, under the steel-gray sky, oblivious to the rhythms of sunrise and sunset, endless, as if they never began, our teeth crack in the cold, we don't want to separate, I can barely swallow, tell me the lyrics of your song, I want to sing with you.

The East Coast lies behind you, pulsing mind, nests of dead birds in which the hardening shells of eggs – stronger than fire and ice – smother the androgynous embryos, you wade through marshes, suffocating fogs and villages of hundred-year-old sages who no longer recognize their gods – their ancestors appearing in nightmares that overwhelm the patient ones living in anonymity, you, strong and calm, journey farther, through endless pine forests, where herds of deer with poisoned blood boiling in their veins stampede toward the vast lakes of the Far North – only to find death in the spears of small, quick hunters, who months earlier rowed out from the frozen spot stitching the continents together, smoothly, without resistance, you slip through the silk curtains of mist, which spread like a dark fleet sailing across the sea, leaving a wake of foam – closing in an instant, along the infinite rivers where the bellies of killed fish glisten, you journey through gorges and canyons, up riverbeds of minerals to the heart of the sacred mountain, a dark place in the middle, glowing silently, a steady force, you breathe on it, touch it, softly, in a scream from the deep – rupturing your eardrum – you hear the moans of your star-crossed companions overcome by eternal sleep, a rock face smoothed by kisses reflects your innocent eyes aglow with sweet pain, the pelvic bones spread, splashing you with salty juices, a volcanic eruption instantly hardening into a shield.

Horses sculpted in black marble. In town squares swept by gusts of winter wind. Rip themselves off their pedestals? No: perhaps they're tempted to go with the boy. The one who woke this morning, serious and dizzy. Woke from sleep overrun by a faint image, blurring. His companions try to keep him from leaving right away. He walks in silence toward the North. Across wheat fields, through birch groves. He won't rest till he reaches the glacier. While he ages like wine. Will he return? Eskimos lead him safely through snowfields and over the Bering Strait. In their boats he sleeps easily. Like anyone would: this is his home. Not that he would erase memory. Only in the glint of frozen water, in crystals and smooth ice does day become bitter enough for him. Only one step — and what was once solid disappears. In the dreams of other men the boy looks calmly over the dark backs of horses and knows what I don't know how to say. Others would need a lifetime. Today, tomorrow, yesterday: it's all the same. I, too, will do what I should have done long ago.

Now, in a bitter or a soft voice, in the lengthened melodies of a lament, in flooding and cracked mirrors, brute force of soldiers and the blind offspring of nomadic animals disturb your sense of reality, which changes like shifting archipelagos in the South Seas, now, in lush cascades of corn, flowing toward a sewer like the pale blood of mortally-wounded dolphins, in moments of horror, before you sink into sleep, which won't release you from the memory of exile, now, when you say *snow* and everything remains the same, in a sad song, slyly imitating the rhythm of a long run across infinity, now, hopelessly, passionately, hastily here, the door ajar, through which water leaks, now, when the walls are closing in and snail shells crack underfoot, now, in the ripe clusters of hail nailing you to the ground, now, at the end and beginning of paths closing, now, in the dark voice coming from the night you shared with everyone lost like you: do you recognize yourself in this poem?

In this moment, in the twilight of a cold room, thunder approaches from a distance, through storm windows and dusty panes, in late afternoon, the water in the pot doesn't boil, when fish gasp under the ice, when half-asleep you tremble, as if without hope, when a pack — a herd of shivering stags leaves the dried marshes deep in the woods and comes to the gardens in town, this fleeting instant, when the cold slices through your spine, when hardened honey cracks in jars, when the thought of a woman's hand — laid on the forehead of the dying — comes closer and closer, when from the depths of memory destroyed villages you wanted to forget begin to rise, when guilt and truth burn your stomach, when frightened pheasants are flushed from tapestries hanging on the wall, when guards leaving their posts whistle to one another, piercing the air, when a sharp stone breaks your skull, should I remind you now that your wounded body will be no different than the shadow a solitary bush casts across the trampled earth, east of Eden?

RADIO: NIGHT PROGRAM

Down the long avenue, grinding sand and tops of chestnuts sinking in a fine suburban mist, along the sidewalk, one foot gliding through the dust, perhaps through cigarette butts, a human figure slowly disappearing into the close of day. Then no one. For a long time. Minutes pass. Maybe, if you listen carefully, a sound, muffled and indistinct, as if a small bell tolled. Maybe just the soft sound of cymbals from a record? *Moonlight in Vermont* by Errol Gardner, blurred by distance, almost a hallucination. Dim blue light, through a veil, fills the cold air. Evening. Puddles of afternoon rain scatter the reflections of passing figures. My face, too. The street evaporates, as if awakening. Not a scream, much less a sigh, can call it back. Did I draw the curtains? I no longer think of people, the last deep drag burning my throat, for the last time I gaze at the empty yard, cut off from the world, in darkness, no exit.

Red bands of earth almost reach the water — stopped by a thin layer of pebbles, the fiery morning winking above, empty, no one around, as if there are no villages near. He undresses slowly, his skin breathes, nostrils widen, muscles quivering, gulping air, his white body glistens as he wades into the shallow water. Waves wash his footprints away, he nearly sinks into the sandy bottom, clumsily tries — again and again — to regain his balance. The water rises around him. Gusts of wind lap the foam against his chest, tiny whirlpools, veined hands, quickened breath, damp forehead. Thick clouds hang above the horizon, muffling the only morning sounds, the sea breeze, screams of gliding gulls, a stone rubbing a stone. He scoops water into his palm and spills a small cascade over his shoulder, watching the drops spray all around him, everywhere. He sees a reflection of distant worlds breaking in the drops, sufferings and journeys, people who passed through him, he calmly exhales, inhales, relaxed and silent as he sinks, letting the water splash his face, a curved wave slipping over his head.

Drowning in twilight just before dawn. Perhaps a harbinger of night? He couldn't make out their footsteps, the way their heels plodded the earth, jackets rubbing against their strong bodies. He longed to hear the squeak of their leather boots. He thought: if my wish isn't granted, I should expect nothing more from life than what fate has already given me. Again he squinted, listened harder, searched his memory — in vain — for tracking skills forgotten long ago: the hunter and the hunted. Worlds overlap, he realized with a start. In the room above him a woman screamed, then her voice burst into broken laughter, neurotic roar.

I'm almost sure I know what you want to say. Follow your hunch, when the time comes. Conjure up an image from thin air — perhaps a timid gesture haunting you from childhood. Don't worry about details added over the years: they're not important. Wherever you are, forget about what happens to you. Think, if you can, of all the ways you say *thou* to someone who should be *you*.

He turned, walked down the short corridor, past the bath-room, the bookshelves no one had used for a long time, entered the kitchen, drew the curtain. Behind the neighbors' door music played softly on the radio, their murmuring a mystery to him. Would you believe he heard someone recit-ing poetry in an empty room? From a distance came the muffled voices of children playing in the street, jumping rope, maybe torturing a kitten. If he paid attention, he could even hear hands swatting a beach ball. He stepped up to the typewriter, to the keys collecting dust since before the war. The milky light in the room suddenly disappeared. No: the sky darkened. A gray cloud, I imagine, covering the shape-less sky, shrouds the city. Before nightfall it's already dark. It's getting colder and colder. The first raindrops plop on the ground. The water trickling down the dusty windows reminds you of a map of unknown lands. Then the world, a blur of shapes and colors, begins to fade, dissolve, disap-pear. He sits and listens calmly to the heavy rains changing the image of everything he knows. Soon, through the sound of spattering rain, he returns to his typewriter, pauses, then starts tapping the keys.

He stands by the open window. Across the empty street dim blue lights glittering in the shop windows, a green light over the entrance to a half-deserted cafe, plaster falling from wet walls, littered sidewalks, two, three people hurrying — home? Absent-mindedly, as if in a movie, he stares toward the end of the street, almost an avenue, with a narrow strip of trampled grass down the middle, almost ruined from so many steps, the weeks' bitter ends, daily heat and nightly frost, monotonous lives and dust, which no longer scatters in the wind. The time: mild evening. Cigarette smoke still pouring into his lungs, he rests without thinking, leaning stoically against the windowsill, as if worn out from work, from demands whose meaning will always remain unknown to him.

LATE EVENING LIGHT

Indifferently, he watched her through the shadows of furniture casually arranged in the narrow room, through a thin curtain drawn across the mirror hanging in the wardrobe, through a shaft of sunlight and dust splitting the room in half. She was fast asleep, head buried under the sheets where the pillow should have been, one shoulder bare, lost to the world. Her hands, her unpolished nails lay on the blanket pulled over her stomach, rising and falling with each breath. Stained sheets, previous guests, other lives. Or was it only his eyes blurring from gazing so long? The curve of her arm covering her dark nipple, the fallen strap of her nightgown. On her shoulder a band of light, as if through a veil, gently slipping over the down below her neck. Maybe he was a little tired. Not impatient. He thought: why here? So many other places, and yet here, always here?

New York City
September 1986

How she stood up on the hill and waved to me. Her lips cold, slightly open, about to say: Where do you come from? It would confuse me. And yet: she would stand still, remembering what never happened, a light breeze lifting tufts of blond hair on her forehead, her hand shielding her eyes from the sun, her firm body breathing in the rhythm of the hill, tense, alert, and waiting, as if there was so much to say. A hidden trail across the field, extending from the foot of the hill. Is it me who wants to feel it under my bare feet, my cautious step? Through closed eyes I see her whispering to herself. Then I flinch at the scream tearing itself free from her throat.

What are you thinking about, she asked him, her face hidden in the shadows cast through the slanted strips of the blinds.

Something I either read or dreamed about. They're one and the same. Let's talk about something else.

Tell me about it, she said, as if she hadn't heard him.

From a distance came the sound of a motorcycle someone was frantically, almost desperately trying to kick start.

Should I tell you? he asked, not expecting an answer.

She drew closer to him, slipping into the armchair, even deeper than before, holding her head in her hands, her elbows propped on her knees. She wasn't touching him. He looked at her.

My story's simple, he said. Do you want me to tell it to you? Even if I do, you won't recognize me. I've already told it many times before. You haven't heard it. Do you really want to hear it once again?

He stared at her, into her eyes. She stared back. Once her eyes were dark, brown, and deep. The whine of the motorcycle echoed in the distance.

An old mansion, almost a palace. An open window. It isn't hot. It isn't hot at all. In the room, half-hidden by a mirror, let's say behind a lead-gray vase full of dried flowers, a woman stands, head gently cocked, as if she's studying the space in front of her. Short hair. A V-neck cotton shirt with a tiny cubic pattern. In the darkness thickening from moment to moment her full breasts glow. No: an outline, just an outline. She contemplates the man sitting at the table, watching him restlessly play with the cigarette lighter on the smooth cloth. Her face drowning in the darkening room. He tries to search for her, his eyes feeling their way over her motionless body, passing over her cheeks and nose, losing himself again and again in her calm breathing.

– Is that the night?

–Yes.

You sleep alone. It happens sometimes. The blue light from the television set. An apple tree blossoming in the dark. You remember everything: the earth, the sea, the sky. Nothing escapes you. You sink into space, which is smaller than dream. Far from the shore melting in your blood, in your beating heart. Dawn breaks over the snows of Argentina. You lie still, on the edge of the world.

For you, M.Š.

I'm watching you, how your fingers glide down your body.
Do you wonder where the angel touched you: your lips, the
back of your knee, your ear? Today, yesterday, even before
that I watched the women of your tribe, how gracefully they
move through rooms, floating, like you, as if on wings,
proud, fearless. I see you clearly. Separate. Come. Come in, I
say.

Another beginning: it doesn't make any sense. I'd rather not even try again. And yet: this image, this faded photograph of you, your sad face, your hands on your lap (do I only imagine it?), in a room with friends — yet not altogether there. The photograph is still here. Along with all the things you wanted then. You know exactly what you believe! How to spend the night, when to bare your shoulders. How carefully you choose your words, which sound so perfect! You talk today, whenever, with anyone. What happened doesn't change anything. The children at your feet play with dominoes made from the bones of animals. Closets filled with smoked glass. Perhaps a book or two. Open on the shelf. Now you can tell me what you kept for years from the ones closest to you. The future's already here. Tell me everything. Ups and downs, the habits of your heart, silences, mild mornings, long-distance calls, sighs, whispers, hopes, fears. I'm no longer here for you to hurt. The gust of autumn wind in the chimes clinking on the balcony: only you can hear it.

A RIVER AND A YOUNG WOMAN

We sit in the shadows of the monastery wall — or what's left of it, the next westbound bus due in half an hour, tears gathering in your eyes — or maybe it just seems that way, I see you crying at the swimming pool, when you were six, washing chlorine from your eyes, how in beautiful abandon your lips and breasts swell, how you sing in a bold voice, in the orange grove whose entrance has been closed to foreigners for decades, thousands and thousands of miles away, on another continent, how you pout when you can't say what you want, like me now, when for the first time I realize I'm not with you, not under the same sky, in the distance the resting workers murmur in Spanish, you shiver, no longer thinking of burning deserts and dream landscapes, places you want to visit before straying too far to return, I lean close to hear what's on your mind: no, I don't know who owns the world — if that's what you're asking, all the other unnecessary encounters disappear from this sequence, your face blurs: my loneliness is the same as yours.

The light in the poem I know by heart spreads over the hills. I'd rather be there, of course. But here, in front of me: a sleeping figure. I don't know who it is. I can only guess: someone who finished a story begun long ago. Someone who knows the difference between speech and silence. Without despair, guilt, glory, hatred. I know his desires, his needs are behind him. He sleeps, but not forever. Fast and sure as the dusk settling on the girl's head, when she hurries home through the cornfields.

For a friend in Zagreb

You write about another time. Like me. Sometimes even better. About men. Women. Memories, which weaken by the hour. About the uneasiness of strangers meeting in visions. Damp darkness over the Alps, in rooms. It's drizzling. Someone we know sets out for Berlin. Cold stars twinkle. We've been locked up for less than half a century, each in his own speech, although we share the same world, the same torments. Does it hurt you as much as it hurts me? Daybreak: what more can I tell you?

A backwoodsman – or maybe only a tight-lipped peasant from the hills bordering an almost inaccessible Alpine village, ancient, I imagine: dejected, but not resigned. The last in his family who can speak to stags, he journeys from his harsh climate, through high and low tides, to a remote village at the northern tip of a Pacific island, the name escapes me, unmapped, lost in the hum of insects, in the labyrinth of overgrown paths and clearings turning back into rain forest, to meet a woman who understands the dialects of fish. At the village entrance, near a loose circle of huts, he sees her wave to him, excited, opening her mouth: no sound. He winces, stops, neck dripping, sweat running down his chest. He stands still: language can't compete with silence. The buzzing midges around his head reveal eternity – the days he spent in front of his house, on the doorstep, up in the hills.

After all, why sadness? Why fear? We don't know the depths of Finnish lakes, the cold of the Siberian taiga, the map of the Gobi desert. We don't even know what's in your dreams. Mine, too. That's the way it is. But you, as always: listening in the dark, lighting matches, gazing straight ahead. The man whose name you won't forget – even in the middle of the night – still hasn't called. You're hungry. In the corner of the room an old man in a rocking chair creaks back and forth, the shining keys of the sax laid on its side reflect your soft face, which you hide from yourself and others. Framed by the window, horses hover above the ground, wandering aimlessly through men's destinies, silk tails sailing in the wind. And for a moment, while the old man leans over a book – leafed through hundreds of times – you see the riders galloping across the fields, through the woods, heads down, black hair waving in the setting sun, the vanishing sun. Gone. Is that why you can't remember the short poem describing the whole world as it was and will be, why dusk blinds you to the stories of everyone, stories known only to the man whose name you won't forget – even in the middle of the night, the man who stands somewhere in the open, alone, in the dark, on the high plains?

WAYS OF SAYING GOODBYE

So winter approaches, she tells herself. Not quite yet, not really, but soon, if I may add. She stares into a river the color of dark olives. Higher up, at the source, it flooded its banks, flooded villages, drowning people and animals. Now it flows calmly. As if nothing happened. The woman I'm describing lies on the hillside: warm ground, a carpet of wildflowers. Her wound sears her. Sometimes she rises absently, and gazes eastward into the distance, and sings sotto voce, splitting the trunks of pines, softening the shuddering hides of deer. She knows no medicine will cure her hope. Above the surface of the water insects, half-frozen, swarm. Only when the wind gusts through the reeds and cloud-packed sky does she wince and for a moment recognize her fear — the way her heart beats only as hard as mine. Only.

On the south side of Malta, where steep cliffs fall into the sea, near stone towers I'm sure men didn't build, there's a garden, unfenced, almost hidden in thick grass, full of sweet-smelling bushes and fine dust settling on his sneakers. In the corner of the garden, where he will never walk again (neither alone nor with the woman who was with him then), a small lake appears, perhaps only a puddle that won't dry. And doesn't reflect his image. It's not important now. I want to say: the plant stems flow with sap, the earth suffers quietly, in the twilight tired eyes rest, sounds fade before the ear can make them out, a storm's brewing, the air vibrates as in the dreams of great painters, the wound continues to burn, swarms of bees buzz above the waves of the sea. I'm afraid the past, the people he lost, can't be translated into sentences with verbs, nor can I summon them back into living memory. I believe that. That's how it happened.

The port grows dark. Across the bay, inmates in the island prison stroke their sweaty bellies. Rain washes the streets, as if before an earthquake. Somewhere two hands clap steadily till morning. In the bus station a boy and a girl have their picture taken. While he stays still. Absent. Mumbling the names of those he loves. In fevered sleep the man next to him turns over on his side, almost raises his head, as if the names he'll never learn to pronounce have stolen into his leaden dreams, and then he sinks back under his blanket. The dull ache in his chest doesn't stop. In the room: perfect peace, aging wooden beams. He tries to cry. Fails. In the bakeries the Chinese start to work.

San Francisco
October 1986

The last thing I remember may be the smell of burnt bread. Now I think it's clear: we'll never end this conversation. I'm leaving. We'll meet again in a few hours, maybe in a few years. Look: a warm handshake, dry palms, thoughtful gaze, no fear, long farewell. I'm leaving you by the unread newspapers. No hard feelings, no sadness. Pigeons coo in the deserted houses on the hill. Everything's as it should be. Through the window boats sail toward the horizon. Damp, heavy air. Sour grass rustling in the corner of the garden. Do you, too, believe I'm walking farther and farther, almost going on a journey? Maybe even to Alaska? Who knows?

At daybreak, as we journeyed through the emerging light, I imagined midwestern prairies covered with snow, empty village squares, buildings without tenants, towns like dying wolves bleeding from slashed bellies, helpless, behind me. On front lawns tattered flags wrapped around flagpoles, brown leaves rotting in the wind, I wonder if the birds were awake at all, sleeping day and night, as if the strong gusts scattering pages of yesterday's newspapers across the squares didn't suit their smooth feathers, too cold for their hollow bones. In thick bushes I wanted to see the gleaming eyes of wild hounds, dense swarms of flies quivering above bare trees, cool reflections in the ponds of freezing frogs, the faces of loved ones lost in time, mothers suckling their babies in the anxiety of morning, packed trains from the suburban ghettos, old men who faint from heavy smells, tears on the cheeks of a blind boy. And I know: the convoy hasn't reached the maternity hospital yet, workers light their first cigarettes in the moment between night and day, no one belongs to anyone, names, dreams, skies filled with stars disappearing.

The river rushes on. As it has for a long time. Herons, or wading birds that look like the herons in field guides, are getting ready to fly south. Reeds rustle in the evening wind, in the breeze off the water. Here and there. The houses lining the bank fade in mist. Pale light fills the windows. Seated by the lamps, people dream of soldiers entering their lives. Sweet apples in their cellars: if no one eats them, they'll begin to rot. A thirteen-year-old girl keeps practicing piano sonatas. Stiff fingers. Steady wind. Hours running on. In everyone's eyes: growing boredom. Think twice. You can also bid farewell. After all, you'll only be changing ways of saying goodbye. I was just like you long ago.

EMPTY ROOMS

Things can't go on like this forever, no words, no shapes, a smeared watercolor. Perhaps it's not too late: somewhere water still spills over the edge of the fountain, somewhere an answer may be found. Let's say a dark flock of sparrows still plays in the yard, a scream returns as an echo, dreams – if they are dreams – never change their meaning, river boats still float with the current. Perhaps it's not too late. That's how I know you can't tell me anything I don't already know. I know I exist. For instance: is this not my own high-pitched voice winding up through the stairways? Is this not my own palm? But why such pain, hope, fear? At once I recognize my own self. Yes, that's me. No doubt about it. That's me.

It could even be a church. Without portals, frescoes, stucco. Smoothly sculpted in brittle stone. Perhaps. As if hauled from a distance, from the unknown into hot desert sand. In this space: I remain as I was. You're the one who changes. The passing hours slowly carry you through February. You're sitting, perhaps all afternoon, under the arches I'm certain a madman dreamed up. The warm sun works its way through the cracks in the ceiling. Specks of light, a whole web glistening on black canvases. I don't know if you can tell the shadows from the wall. Holding your breath. Utterly still. The outlines of the faces you met and forgot, your brothers and sisters, the Russian steppe you traveled over so many times, all blur together, all disappear. Calm fills the air, as if in the mountains. Perhaps muffled voices, even humming – it's true – coming from somewhere. Empty echoes. Sinking into you. Softening you until you're completely changed. Alive to passion. Longing. The chirping of a titmouse. How you paired off to walk across the Karst high meadows to the sea. (In a way you're still walking.) That whisper, I can't tell what it is: singing dervishes from Konya? A half-finished poem by a Romanian, who will die far from the shores of the Danube, filled with nostalgia? Besides, what interests me is you – sinking into dusk. Your face buried in your hands. You see nothing. Your eyes will open only when day comes to an end. And you'll be older, years older, though the monks living here would tell you only a moment has passed. You'll be old enough to recognize a thing or two: a love that lasts longer than any separation.

Rothko Chapel
Houston
February 1988

The guts of the cuttlefish water down its ink. Birdcall in low clouds. Probably a windhover. The sunbaked blocks of stone begin to cool. Summer thaws. Sweet smell of a cicada's broken wing. And you — where are you in this vision? Do you stare through waves of reeds? If it's really you, then you aren't talking to the man by your side. Leaning forward, as if in the middle of a field, he wants to know what catches your eye. Focused on the horizon. Glistening in the dark, as if before a storm. No worse than the shadows trembling on the walls of your room, the horrifying portraits of a stranger drawn by twilight. This moment won't pass. Ever. A boy runs over sand dunes. Does he know language offers many words for the same thing?

The image — lost forever — comes to life again. Always the same room, embedded in darkness. Flies on the cracked walls. In the stale air, the smell of stomach acids and urine. A child immersed in a picture book of exotic plants, frozen in an endless moment. A blue labyrinth of veins shines through his white skin. Was he raised in love by Albanian women in the damp and dark? A face bitterness turned pale. Dry pears on the windowsill. Still life. The sand in the hourglass turns into dust. Someday, somewhere, perhaps this boy, now at rest, will become a man who travels, cries, causes pain. Who will think of home only when he catches a reflection of eyes — as lonely as ours — staring back at him from mirrors, sand, and grass. Doubts will ravage him. Visions of abandoned ports, pride, drunkenness — everything will haunt him.

The dripping tap. Keepsakes in the drawer. Glowing coals. The cat's nest on a friend's bed. The sky comes down. Fruit rots in the grass. Bruised by September. Abstracted, you stroll down the back streets, through the coastal village. The port drifts off to sleep, moaning in terror. In bare feet you feel the earth, every stone, every plant. Time, unspent, hardens in the bronze bells of the cathedral. Another strange sound, like the sigh of a sick child in early evening, vanishes into nothingness, into history. Are you coming? Going? Your hand's half-raised to greet or wave goodbye, like this:

In this humidity, mosquitoes swarming above the cotton fields that must sprawl beyond the levees, I lean against an ancient pillar, imagining on this porch a woman who longed for Paris, halfway to the noisy port, to the delta where ships from the East no longer anchor, the babble of young travelers, I turn my back on them with ease, memory leaves me only a snatch of the blues the blind black man sang yesterday in a bar, the smell of the palm trees in a garden hidden from the house I'm staying in comforts me. So now I think of you, serious boy, troubled friend, name fading on a gravestone. How you wrote of flowers changing shape when sadness overcomes them. Of taxi drivers, places you didn't visit, love untouched by time – and those who understand that: like you and me.

New Orleans
December 1988

SKETCHES FOR THE RETURN

Early morning. A green river. Nameless. Cold muse above the famous statue. In a museum: neolithic coins exhibited as gold. The light in the university library. I think about a young mother, who reads and reads and doesn't write any letters, sitting up late, poring over another book, her throat sore from smoking. Empty parking lots. Mansions in a ring around the castle: they'd like to dream in German. If it weren't so cold, the laundry would hang from the balconies. Last year's grapes rot on the cobblestones, in front of the cathedral. Through the window, fog and clouds, someone stares at the pampas overseas. Nothing happened to him. Not for half a century or even longer. Someone else, deepened by drink, hurrying across the empty marketplace to lose himself forever in his studio, is probably not a gift from God, neither to himself nor to others. I only mention him because without his wandering I couldn't describe anything. In the basement of an old house an all-night bar is open. Yet at this hour only a cluttered counter, unwashed glasses, air thick with marijuana. Two asleep in a seedy corner. Separate. Someone I know would probably say: loneliness — that's crazy. Yet, in fact, that's how it should be. In you, small town, the years don't leave any marks: they just slip by unseen. I, too, am as I was before. Even this sweet voice, which has already faded away (perhaps a singer practicing for nothing) can be sure these are the lungs I use to breathe, this the air I turn into song.

Ashes in the air, like a cloth hanging in stifling heat, people can barely breathe, the Presbyterian bell tolls five in the afternoon, the sky settles on the ground, a frightened girl hesitates as she climbs into a taxi, goodbye unsteamed mirrors. Unread books, flakes of rust falling from fire escapes, thirty-year-olds on a street corner stubbing their cigarettes out on the brick wall, sweat trickling down their spines, dogs tossing and turning in their sleep, water stagnating in the pipes, moments dragging on and on. Longer. Even longer. Under layers of leaves swarms of insects suffocate. Cracks widen in the wall. Don't you think there's a certain beauty in the way the distant glow of the fire – consuming villages in the south – trembles above the rolling hills, far from the town neither you nor I want to leave?

Look again, she told him. Look carefully.
He thought: Once more I start from the beginning . . . with
the rolling roofs of houses packed tightly together, the sun's
reflection in the magnifying glass a boy uses to burn a small
lizard, a surprisingly clear sky, a child walking on the para-
pet of the Three Bridges, a group of short skirts playing
hopscotch in front of the projects, the sagging banks of the
river that runs to the sewer, a gentle voice vibrating in his
mind, trees slumping over in the city park . . . the first
dreams in airless cellars, a red-haired girl who's counting to
a hundred, leaning her forehead against a wall, he imagines
her running barefoot up the street to the main post office,
outside time, simple beauty of love and things for which
other languages have no words – pine needles in a glass pot
on the windowsill, loneliness buried in memory . . .
So I always return, he told himself. I never left. Thus he
brought to an end his line of thought, metaphor, yearning,
the whole world.

Your story's simple. You won't see many loved ones when you return, like an otter surfacing in a lake to catch its breath. You won't find words for short greetings, the seasons, unsuccessful missions, white phosphorus lighting the passion in soldiers' eyes, a distant whistle on steep hillsides you never climbed, children's cane baskets floating silently across a river basin, the way you have a constant burning pain, the constellations discovered in a premonition, Oriental love songs, the disappointment of everything we were and will be. Believe me: this is your story. Later, I'll tell it again — only better.

About the Author

Aleš Debeljak is considered by critics to be one of the premier poets of Central Europe. Born in 1961 in Slovenia, which was, before it became an independent state in 1991, the northernmost republic of Yugoslavia, he received a degree in comparative literature and an M.A. in cultural studies from the University of Ljubljana and a Ph.D. in Social Thought from Syracuse University in Syracuse, New York. He has held writing fellowships from the Virginia Center for the Creative Arts and Cambridge University, Great Britain.

He has published four books of poetry, three books of cultural criticism, and edited an anthology of American short stories in his native Slovenia. His numerous awards include the prestigious Prešeren Prize, which is the Slovenian National Book Award, and the Hayden Carruth Poetry Prize.

His work has been translated into many languages including Serbo-Croatian, Polish, Italian, German, Dutch, Lithuanian, French, Hungarian, Spanish, and English. He writes a regular column for a Slovenian cultural fortnightly, *Razgledi (Viewpoints)*, and for *Literatur und Kritik*, an Austrian literary magazine, as well as working as an editor for the publishing house Wieser. He edited the Slovenian, Croatian, and Serbian section for *Shifting Borders: East European Poetries in the '80s* (Fairleigh Dickinson University Press, 1993) and is an editor of *Prisoners of Freedom: Contemporary Slovenian Poetry* (Pedernal Press, Santa Fe, NM, 1994).

His work frequently appears in literary journals in the United States. He is currently a professor of cultural studies at the University of Ljubljana and is an active member of a Slovenian P.E.N. Center.

About the Translator

Poet and translator Christopher Merrill is the author of three volumes of poetry, *Workbook* (Teal Press, 1988), *Fevers & Tides* (Teal Press, 1989), and *Watch Fire,* forthcoming from White Pine Press in 1994. Editor of the Peregrine Smith Poetry Series, he recently edited a collection entitled *The Forgotten Language: Contemporary Poets and Nature* (Peregrine Smith, 1991). Other books by Mr. Merrill include *The Grass of Another Country: A Journey Through the World of Soccer* (Holt, 1993) and the forthcoming *Only the Nails Remain: Three Balkan Journeys.*

He was selected by W. S. Merwin to receive the 1993 Lavan Younger Poet Award from the Academy of American Poets. He lives in Portland, Oregon, where he makes his living as a freelance journalist.